Contents

You can find words in bold, **like this**, in the Glossary.

No Sun, no weather!

It is very easy to take the Sun for granted, but to do so is a mistake. The Sun is the power behind the weather. Without it there would be no sunshine, rain, wind, fog or hail. In fact, life on Earth would end.

The Sun is also important because of the way in which it causes day and night and the seasons. This means that each area of the world has weather patterns which repeat themselves again and again. This gives each place its different **climate**. Weather is monitored from day to day, whereas climate is the pattern of the weather over a long period of time.

It is important to know about the Sun because it affects the way we live. And, as we shall see, it plays a part in the formation of clouds.

Artists have often shown clouds in their pictures. The artist John Constable was famous for his paintings of skies. This picture is called Chain Pier, Brighton. *Often, the sky was given as much space as the rest of the picture put together.*

Clouds

To many people, clouds are a mystery. They think that learning to identify them would be too complicated. This is not true. There are simple ways of sorting clouds to help identify them. Once you know what the different clouds are, you will be able to find out what sort of weather they are likely to bring.

Weather symbols

In professional weather reports, the weather is shown on maps with a set of symbols that are internationally recognised. This means that **data** can be shared by **meteorologists** around the world. By sharing data, a wider picture of the weather can be built up, so that it can be predicted more efficiently. Sometimes, different symbols are used for weather reports on television, in newspapers, and on the Internet. These are more like pictures and can easily be understood by the public.

Be careful!

Do not look directly at the Sun when studying the weather. Never shelter under trees during a thunderstorm, as they may be hit by lightning.

These are the internationally recognised symbols used to represent clouds.

Weather symbols: clouds

■ Cloud coverage		■ Cloud types	
◯	no clouds	⌐⌐	cirrus
⦶	⅛ or less	—	stratus
◔	⅜	⌣	stratocumulus
		⌂	cumulus
◑	4⁄8	⌓	cumulonimbus with anvil
		∠	altostratus
◕	6⁄8	⌣⌣	altocumulus
		2	cirrostratus
●	overcast	⌣⌣	cirrocumulus
⊗	sky obscured	⦟	nimbostratus

What is the Sun?

Where does the Sun come from? Scientists think our universe was made through a process called the **big bang**, between 10 and 20 billion years ago. When this happened, the Sun was formed out of billions of swirling particles of dust. It is approximately five billion years old and has enough energy to last another five billion years. Fortunately this means that the Sun will be with us for a long time yet.

The Sun is the source of all our natural light. It gives us our daytime. Without the Sun, we would all freeze to death. Sunlight is also reflected off the moon at night, giving moonlight. The Sun looks relatively big to us because it is only 150 million kilometres (93 million miles) away. Light from it only takes eight minutes to reach us. Compared to this, light from the nearest bright star (Alpha Centauri A) takes four years, even though light travels at 299,972 kilometres (186,282 miles) per second!

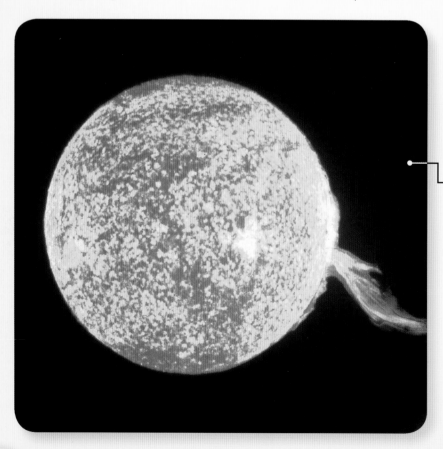

Did you know that our Sun is about 1.4 million kilometres (864,000 miles) in diameter? It is about five billion years old and the temperature at its core is 15 million °C (59 million °F).

SUNSHINE
AND CLOUDS
REVISED AND UPDATED

Measuring the Weather

Alan Rodgers and Angella Streluk

Heinemann
LIBRARY

www.heinemann.co.uk/library
Visit our website to find out more information about Heinemann Library books.

To order:
☎ Phone 44 (0) 1865 888066
📄 Send a fax to 44 (0)1865 314091
💻 Visit the Heinemann Library Bookshop at www.heinemann.co.uk/library to browse our catalogue and order online.

First published in Great Britain by Heinemann Library, Halley Court, Jordan Hill, Oxford OX2 8EJ, part of Harcourt Education.
Heinemann Library is a registered trademark of Harcourt Education Ltd.

Editorial: Joanna Talbot
Design: Michelle Lisseter and Philippa Jenkins
Picture Research: Ruth Blair
Production: Julie Carter

Originated by Chroma Graphics
Printed and bound in China by South China Printing Company Limited

ISBN 978 0 431 03855 1
12 11 10 09 08
10 9 8 7 6 5 4 3 2 1

British Library Cataloguing in Publication Data
Rodgers, Alan
    Sunshine and clouds. - (Measuring the weather)
    1. Sunshine - Measurement - Juvenile literature
    2. Clouds
    Measurement - Juvenile literature
    I. Title II. Streluk, Angella
    5 5 1 . 5 ' 2 7 1
A full catalogue record for this book is available from the British Library.

Acknowledgements
The publishers would like to thank the following for permission to reproduce photographs: Bruce Coleman Collection: pp. **11**, **24**; Eye Ubiquitous/NASA p. **10**; FLPA p. **28**; GeoScience Features pp. **20**, **22**, **26** (pics 1, 2, 4); Getty Images/Stone p. **16**; K E Woodley/The Met Office p. **18**; R N Hughes/The Met Office p. **23**; Robert Harding Picture Library pp. **6**, **25**; Science Photo Library pp. **21**, **26** (pics 3, 6); Stone p**7**; T J Lawson/The Met Office p. **26** (pic 5); The Art Archive p. **4**; Topham Picturepoint p. **13**; Trevor Clifford Photography pp. **8**, **15**.

Cover photographs reproduced with permission of Science Photo Library and Photodisc.

Our thanks to Jacquie Syvret of the Met Office for her assistance during the preparation of this book.

Every effort has been made to contact copyright holders of any material reproduced in this book. Any omissions will be rectified in subsequent printings if notice is given to the publishers.

Disclaimer
All the Internet addresses (URLs) given in this book were valid at the time of going to press. However, due to the dynamic nature of the Internet, some addresses may have changed, or sites may have changed or ceased to exist since publication. While the author and publishers regret any inconvenience this may cause readers, no responsibility for any such changes can be accepted by either the author or publishers.

The Sun is like a giant engine that causes our weather. As the Earth turns, the half that faces the Sun warms up. The other half cools down. Because the Earth is curved, some parts, especially the **equator**, are warmed up more than others. Land and sea also absorb heat at different rates. All of these things cause hot air to rise and cold air to sink in different places and at different times. This process gives us our winds.

Thermals

The Sun heating up the Earth can cause heat to rise in currents called **thermals**. On warm, sunny days, these produce **cumulus** clouds (see pages 20–21). As the Sun heats the air, moisture rises in the sky until it cools and **condenses**. This produces clouds that look very white and bright in the sunshine because the moisture reflects sunlight very well. The fluffy cumulus clouds do not last for a very long time.

Like some birds, this glider uses thermals to give it lift. It does not have an engine to help lift it higher into the sky. The pilot looks for tell-tale signs of thermals, such as fluffy cumulus clouds. Pilots also know where thermals are most likely to rise. These include above wheat fields and roof tops in the afternoon.

The Sun and temperature

The temperature is not the same all around you. Even within a small area, temperatures are different. The main difference is between shade and direct sunshine. This is why professional **meteorologists** always measure temperatures in the shade. They can then compare their **data** knowing that they are all measuring it in the same way. Clouds form their own shade, which reduces the temperature.

The Sun causes changes in temperature. About 19 percent of the heat from the Sun is absorbed by the **atmosphere** and clouds. Some 51 percent of the heat is absorbed into the Earth's surface. About 30 percent of all the heat from the Sun is reflected back into space.

The Earth is a **sphere**, which means that the Sun's rays fall more directly onto the **equator**. Towards the **poles**, the curve of the Earth means the rays strike it at an angle. The rays become more spread out, and the heat is less intense. Where the Sun's rays are more concentrated, it will be hotter.

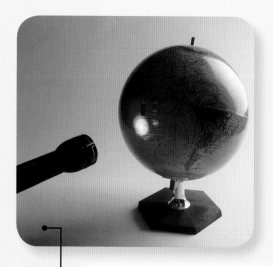 

You can use a torch and model globe to show the different amounts of sunlight that different parts of the world receive. When the torch is shone onto the nearest part of the globe, the circle of light will be small. If the light is shone near the top of the globe, it will become a shape called an ellipse. The light leaving the torch is the same, but the area it is spread over gets bigger or smaller. So it is with sunlight on the Earth.

The greenhouse effect

Even though much heat is lost through the atmosphere, the Earth stays warm because of the **"greenhouse effect"**. Special gases called "greenhouse gases" keep heat in the atmosphere. Without these gases, the temperature on Earth would be much colder than it is. Many scientists are worried that humans have increased the amount of greenhouse gases in the atmosphere. This means more heat has been trapped, upsetting the delicate balance of Earth's atmosphere.

Carbon dioxide is one of the greenhouse gases. It is released when **fossil fuels** are burned. The gases used in some refrigerators and aerosol cans have also been linked to the increase in greenhouse gases.

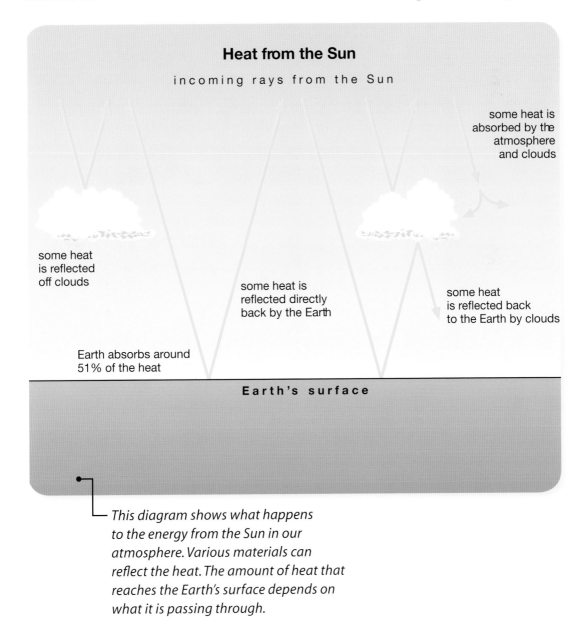

Heat from the Sun

incoming rays from the Sun

some heat is absorbed by the atmosphere and clouds

some heat is reflected off clouds

some heat is reflected directly back by the Earth

some heat is reflected back to the Earth by clouds

Earth absorbs around 51% of the heat

Earth's surface

This diagram shows what happens to the energy from the Sun in our atmosphere. Various materials can reflect the heat. The amount of heat that reaches the Earth's surface depends on what it is passing through.

Day and night

As the Earth rotates, places travel into sunlight and then into shadow. This gives day and night respectively. The change in temperature caused by night and day makes the weather very complicated. Also, land and sea heat up and cool down at different rates. During the day, the land warms up more quickly than the sea. At night, the sea cools down quite slowly compared to the land. On a warm summer's day, this produces a breeze that moves from the sea to the land. At night, after a sunny day in the summer, the breeze moves from the land to the sea.

Temperature usually rises during the day and falls during the night. This rise and fall is affected by the presence of clouds. During the day, clouds can stop sunlight from reaching the Earth, making it cooler. However, at night the clouds act like a blanket and keep in the warmth of the Earth. They stop this warmth from escaping into space, which prevents the temperature falling sharply.

You can see day and night clearly in this picture. On the far right, it is midday. On the far left, it is midnight. Earth is always turning. In this picture, it is turning to the right. Is it sunrise or sunset on the line dividing day from night?

Day, night, and clouds

On a warm sunny day, heat coming off the Earth can force air upwards in **thermals**. If this air contains enough moisture, it will form fluffy **cumulus** clouds when it reaches a cold enough layer of air. These clouds appear and disappear on a warm sunny day. At night, there is no sunlight warming the land and making thermals. In Antarctica, the very cold temperature on the ground also does not produce thermals. Therefore cumulus type clouds do not form there.

Dew and frost

When there is no sunshine or clouds, it can be cold enough for frost and fog. After the Sun has gone down, it gets cooler and the temperature of the ground falls. As the temperature of the air falls, drops of water called dew form on the grass. Dew is formed when the **water vapour** in the air **condenses** as it touches cool surfaces. If it is very cold, the drops of water will turn straight into **ice crystals**. When this happens we have a **hoar frost**.

These drops of water were not caused by rain. Water vapour in the air has turned back into water as the temperature has dropped. It is called dew.

UV radiation

We can all see the light that comes from the Sun, but the Sun's rays also contain ultraviolet (UV) **radiation**. This UV radiation contains a lot of energy. Some of it is harmful to living things. Almost all the most harmful UV radiation is absorbed on its journey through the **atmosphere**. The rest reaches the Earth and has an effect on living things, including humans.

UV radiation causes skin to react and produce a tan to protect itself. Some people tan more easily than others. Those who do not tan easily may have their skin burnt more quickly by UV radiation. Even those who do tan may receive a harmful dose of UV rays while tanning. UV radiation causes skin cancer, and can make skin wrinkle at an earlier age. Whilst it may look attractive to have a tan, it is not worth risking your health for.

The UV Index

The UV Index shows what form of protection you need against the Sun. The readings are given on a scale of 1 to 10+. Weather forecasts on television and in newspapers include maps showing these readings. Use the chart to find out whether you are likely to damage your skin or not (you need to know what skin type you have). "Low" means that there is little risk of burning or damaging your skin. "Very high" means that it is almost certain that you will burn, so you should stay out of the sun.

Exposure levels and their risks to different skin types					
UV Index number	Exposure level	Fair skin which burns	Fair skin which tans	Brown skin	Black skin
1–2	Minimal	Low	Low	Low	Low
2–4	Low	Medium	Low	Low	Low
5	Medium	High	Medium	Low	Low
6	Medium	Very High	Medium	Medium	Low
7	High	Very High	High	Medium	Medium
8	High	Very High	High	Medium	Medium
9	High	Very High	High	Medium	Medium
10+	Very High	Very High	High	High	Medium

BE SAFE!

Avoid the effects of UV radiation:

- Don't spend too much time in the sun between 10:00 am and 4:00 pm.
- Work or play in the shade whenever you can.
- Wear sunscreen of at least SPF (Sun Protection Factor) 15 – even in the shade.
- Wear a hat with a wide brim.
- Wear tightly woven full-length clothing.
- Wear UV protective sunglasses.

Remember that even when you are in the shade, pavements, grass, and sand can reflect the Sun's UV radiation on to you. How is this boy protecting himself from the Sun's strong rays?

What are clouds?

People are usually interested in which clouds bring rain.
However, there are many types of clouds, and not all of them
bring rain. Knowing about clouds makes it easier to forecast the weather.

A cloud is formed when moist (damp) air cools. Weather happens in a particular
part of the **atmosphere**. The higher you go in this part of the atmosphere, the
cooler it gets. In dry air, there is a 1 °C (34 °F) drop in temperature for every
100 metres (328 feet) you go up. As the air cools, the **water vapour** in the air
condenses around tiny particles of salt or pollutants, forming water droplets.
Along with billions of others, these droplets make up a cloud.

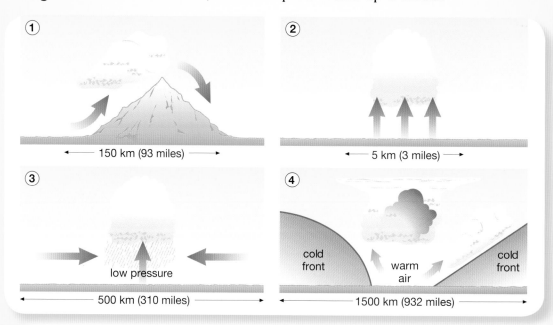

① ←— 150 km (93 miles) —→

② ←— 5 km (3 miles) —→

③ low pressure ←— 500 km (310 miles) —→

④ cold front — warm air — cold front ←— 1500 km (932 miles) —→

*There are four main ways in which clouds are formed. All of them involve
water vapour being forced higher in the sky where it is cooler.*

1 *"Relief" topography or "mountain" cloud. Clouds and rain can be produced
   by moist air being "forced" up by obstacles such as hills or mountains.*

2 ***Convectional** clouds. Heat rising from the ground forces moist air up.
   These events are called **thermals** and are a good source of clouds. They
   are called convectional clouds because rising heat is known as convection.*

3 ***Convergence** of air. Clouds are formed when air meets from opposite
   directions and is forced upwards. This is called convergence.*

4 *Lifting air along **weather fronts**. Weather fronts, which occur when
   different temperature **air masses** meet, force air upwards. Clouds are
   produced and they often bring rain.*

If there are so many ways in which clouds are produced, how do we ever see clear blue skies? When the sky is blue, especially in the summer, there may be high **air pressure**. High air pressure means the air above is sinking down. This means that air cannot rise and cool, so clouds will not form.

TRY THIS YOURSELF!

You can make your own cloud in a large plastic bottle. (Make sure you ask an adult to help you with this project.)

- Put some water into your container. Shake the bottle to mix the air and water.
- Get an adult to strike a match and put it into the bottle. The water will extinguish the flame.
- Tighten the lid. Squeeze and release the bottle. What do you see?

Shaking the bottle mixes air and water, putting water vapour into the air. The smoke provides tiny particles for the cloud to form around.

Cloud cover

When recording the weather, there is a big difference between a sky with a few small clouds and an **overcast** sky. There are several ways of recording the total amount of cloud cover. One popular system is based on mentally dividing the whole visible sky into eighths or **oktas** (divide the sky in half, in half again, and then in half once more). In the United States, the system is based on tenths of the sky.

The table below shows how cloud cover can be calculated. The terms in the "Description" column are for use by non-experts. On weather forecasts, these are usually illustrated with sun and cloud symbols that show how much sun and cloud there is.

Cloud cover			
Amount of sky covered	Oktas (eighths)	Tenths	Description
Clear sky	0	0	Sunny
One quarter of sky	2	2 to 3	More sunny than cloudy
One half of sky	4	5	Partly sunny
Three quarters of sky	6	7 to 8	More cloudy than sunny
Full sky	8	10	Overcast

It is surprising how much of the sky is obscured if you are standing near to a building. This could give an inaccurate idea of how much cloud there is. Walk out into an open space and look all round, concentrating on how much cloud is in the sky.

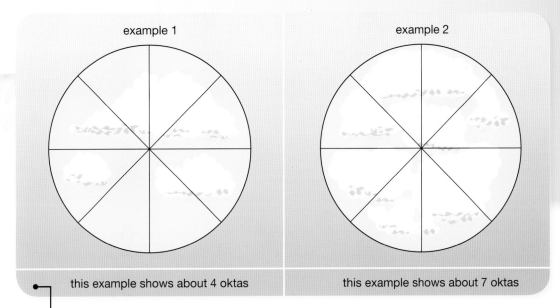

example 1

example 2

this example shows about 4 oktas

this example shows about 7 oktas

These diagrams give examples of the sky as you might see it. The cloud can be scattered all over the sky. The lines shown here show you how to divide the sky up into the correct number of portions. To work out the cloud cover you need to decide how many of them would be full if all the clouds were put together.

Recording cloud cover

Cloud cover is measured as near to 9:00 a.m. as possible. When recording cloud cover, you must stand where there is a clear view of the sky. Stand away from buildings and other obstacles. If the sky is hidden by fog, record that there is "obscured sky".

If the clouds are spread out in the sky, try to imagine how much they would cover if they were placed all together. This needs a little practice. Remember not to look directly at the Sun. You can make two recordings each day. In the winter, the second recording is taken at night. In this case, you could work out the amount of cloud by looking at the parts of the sky where you can see stars.

In some places, the light from street lights reflected on the clouds shows up the areas covered by cloud. Professional **meteorologists** shine spotlights or lasers on the clouds to work out how high up they are.

Cloud classification

In science, it is important to name things. In 1803, Luke Howard, a British scientist, suggested names for the different types of clouds. His system had four basic cloud forms, which used Latin words to describe what he saw: **stratus** (layers), **cumulus** (heaps), **cirrus** (wisps of hair), and **nimbus** (violent rain). These words could be combined into a single name. For example, stratocumulus is a layered and lumpy cloud. In 1887, two scientists called Ralph Abercromby and Hugh Hildebrand Hildbrandsson expanded Howard's system. This is the system **meteorologists** still use today.

There are ten main types of clouds. Each type is classed into one of the three main height levels that clouds are found at in the sky. These are high, middle, and low clouds. Cumulonimbus clouds can be seen at more than one level.

Luke Howard (1772–1864) created his system for naming clouds after studying them for a long time. His system makes understanding cloud names much easier. If a separate name had to be learnt for each of the ten clouds, it would be much harder.

Cloud types

The ten main cloud types are shown, with their abbreviations, in the chart below.

Main cloud types				
Height	**Stratus clouds** (layers)	**Cumulus clouds** (heaps)		**Other clouds**
High level 5,000–13,000m (16,400–43,000 feet)	Cirrostratus (**C**s)	Cirrocumulus (**C**c) (cirriform)	Cumulonimbus (**Cb**)	Cirrus (**C**i)
Middle level 2,000–7,000m (6,600–23,000 feet)	Altostratus (**A**s) Nimbostratus (**N**s)	Altocumulus (**A**c) (alto)		
Low level 0–2,000m (0–6,600 feet)	Stratus (**S**t) (stratiform)	Cumulus (**C**u) Stratocumulus (**S**c)		

The first part of the names of these clouds may help you to work out how high they are in the sky. The rest of the word may help you work out the way the cloud looks. In brackets are the abbreviations which meteorologists use on their data recording sheets. It would be hard for them to fit in the full names of the different cloud types into the tiny boxes on their sheets! You can find out more about these clouds on the following pages.

How high are clouds?

It is difficult to work out the height and size of clouds. This is especially so with cirrocumulus and altocumulus clouds. Experienced weather watchers use the fingers of their outstretched arm as a guide. If you can only cover individual clouds with one finger, you are looking at cirrocumulus clouds. They are small clouds which look even smaller because they are high up. If it takes three fingers to cover a cloud you are looking at altocumulus clouds. These are larger and in the middle level height.

At the **polar** regions, each cloud type is found much lower in the sky than shown in the chart. In the **tropical** regions, each type is found much higher.

Cumuliform clouds

When young children are asked to produce a picture of clouds, they often draw a lumpy shape. This is what cumuliform or **cumulus** clouds look like. They are made up of small heaps of cloud, with clear edges and flat bottoms, which show up against the blue sky. Cumulus clouds are not always white. They can also be many shades of grey. Cumulus clouds are often formed on hot summer days, when heat rises and reaches the cold air high up. They disappear as they **evaporate** again.

When they are low in the sky, cumulus clouds have three basic shapes. Cumulus humilis is rather flat-bottomed and wider than it is tall. It is a fair-weather cloud. However, it can grow into cumulus mediocris. This is as tall as it is wide. This might grow into cumulus congestus, which is taller than it is wide. (See photographs of these on page 26.) These last clouds can produce moderate to heavy showers. They can mean that cold weather is approaching. Beware, they may be followed by cumulonimbus storm clouds!

*Fires can cause clouds of **condensation** to appear in the sky. When a fire is burning its way through forests and countryside, the smoke merges with the clouds to make special clouds called pyrocumulus clouds.*

Sometimes, cumulus clouds are very high up in the sky and grouped together into waves of clouds, called cirrocumulus. Each individual cloud is quite small. They are so high in the cold sky that they are not made of **water vapour**, but **ice crystals**.

Bad weather cumulus clouds

You would not want to spend too long outside under cumulus clouds that have joined together into huge coverings of clouds called stratocumulus. They are dull blankets of cloud that form when the tops of the clouds rise and spread out sideways. Unless they are very thick they will bring only drizzle or light **precipitation**.

Not all cumuliform clouds are harmless. Some can develop into the rain-bearing cumulonimbus. This cloud brings violent hail, thunder and lightning, as we shall see on page 26.

The altocumulus, or mackerel sky, is made of layered clouds with waves that are like the pattern on the mackerel fish. These clouds sometimes show that a change in the weather is approaching.

Stratiform clouds

Stratiform (**stratus**) clouds are made up of layers of unbroken cloud, which have a flat base. These are often white in the sky. Nimbostratus, altostratus, and cirrostratus clouds appear in the lower, middle, and upper parts of the sky. Stratus clouds are found at all levels of the sky. When stratiform cloud appears in the lowest level of the sky, it brings drizzle or, if it's cold enough, snow.

Stratus clouds can be formed from moist air that has not risen very far into the sky. Sometimes, buildings on hills can be covered by stratus clouds! This shows how low they can be. Stratus clouds can be so thin that they will not block out the Sun. Because of this, care should be taken not to look directly at the Sun through this cloud. Sometimes, this low cloud becomes lumpy and patchy all over. Then it is called stratocumulus. This is a layer of **cumulus** clouds.

*Stratus is both a cloud itself and a type of cloud. This grey sky is a layer of stratus, situated in the lowest level of the **atmosphere**. This stratus can bring drizzle.*

Other types of stratus cloud

Cirrostratus is a very high cloud. It is cold and made out of **ice crystals**. It is very pale, smooth, and thin. When cirrostratus only covers part of the sky, the other part of the sky often has other cirrus clouds.

Altostratus is found in the middle level of the sky. It is thicker than cirrostratus and made of water droplets. The cloud is greyish or bluish in colour. It can be thin enough for the Sun to shine weakly through it, but it covers the Sun enough to stop it from casting any shadows.

If cloud is so thick and dark that it blots out the Sun, and rain or snow is falling, then the cloud is nimbostratus.

*Cirrostratus is very thin, but the beautiful circle made by the moonlight shining through shows that it contains a fine layer of ice crystals. The cloud is so thin that the **halo** around the moon is sometimes the only clue that the cloud is there. Altostratus cloud is far easier to see. It is lower in the sky and is made up of water droplets instead of ice crystals. It does not produce halos.*

Cirriform clouds

Cirriform (**cirrus**) clouds can be among the most beautiful of clouds to look at as they flow and form in the sky. On a nice day, sadly, they are strong indicators that a change in the weather is coming.

Cirrus clouds are high up in the sky, where the temperature is extremely cold and the winds are very fast. They are made up of water, in the form of millions of **ice crystals** that are stretched out across the sky. The direction of the streaks of the clouds shows which way the wind is blowing at this level of the sky. The word cirrus comes from Latin. It means "wisp of hair".

Cirrus uncinus is a beautiful type of cirriform cloud. These clouds were thought to look like the tails of female horses. They were given the name "Mares' Tails" because of this.

Types of cirrus cloud

One form of cirrus cloud is cirrus uncinus. At the end of these streaks of cloud is an upturned "hook". Ice crystals in the air begin to drop, but the strong winds below them blow them into long streaks. The "hooks" show the point where the crystals began to drop. The streaks show the direction in which the wind was travelling.

Cirrostratus is high, very even, thin layered cloud. It often covers much of the sky. There are two sorts of cirrostratus cloud. Cirrostratus fibratus is created by continuous strong winds. It looks long and has thin lines that spread out across the sky. Cirrostratus nebulosis is made by gentle rising air. This cloud is hard to see, but when the Sun shines through it at the right angle, you can see a **halo** around the Sun.

Sometimes, you can spot aeroplanes easily in the clear blue sky. This is because their hot exhaust fumes produce long, thin, white cirrus clouds called contrails. They often disappear quickly, but they can last up to 30 minutes when there is a lot of moisture high in the sky.

*These are clouds which are caused by people. They are formed when **water vapour** from aircraft engines **condenses**. Sometimes planes make holes in clouds. The holes are called distrails.*

Giant clouds

The real giant of the cloud kingdom is cumulonimbus **incus**.
It is the biggest cloud of all. The storm that it brings can release as
much energy as an atomic bomb. The cloud grows in stages. Sometimes
cold, heavy air forces warm air to rise up quickly. This causes a rapid
and violent change in the weather. This is when **cumulus** clouds are
formed. These may then develop into giant clouds.

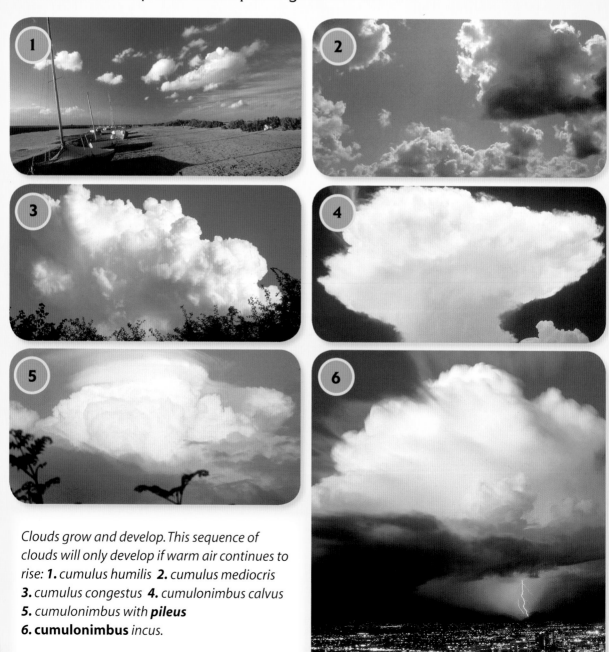

*Clouds grow and develop. This sequence of
clouds will only develop if warm air continues to
rise:* **1.** *cumulus humilis* **2.** *cumulus mediocris*
3. *cumulus congestus* **4.** *cumulonimbus calvus*
5. *cumulonimbus with* **pileus**
6. cumulonimbus *incus.*

The cloud sequence

Cumulus humilis (1) and cumulus mediocris (2) would not spoil a picnic! However, cumulus congestus (3) develops when there are strong **updraughts** of warm air with cold air above, which causes **turbulence.** Cumulonimbus calvus (4), the next stage, is a big, white cloud, up to 9,000 metres (30,000 feet) high. These clouds bring moderate to heavy showers, and strong winds.

Cumulonimbus with pileus (5), is a giant cloud 6,000–9,000 metres (20,000–30,000 feet) high. If the updraught of air grows stronger, it blows the top off a cumulonimbus calvus cloud, producing a "cap", or smooth flat top. The cumulonimbus calvus cloud then grows and catches up with this "cap". This cloud means the weather is going to turn nasty.

Cumulonimbus incus (6) is the last stage, bringing rain, strong winds, and even tornadoes. At 18,000 metres (60,000 feet) tall, it is so big it would make Mount Everest look small! Hail is also produced in this cloud. Hail is made of ice particles that travel up and down inside the cloud. They melt and re-freeze until they become so heavy that they fall to the ground.

Cumulonimbus incus also produces thunder and lightning. Negative and positive electrical energy travels back and forth between the cloud and the ground. This is lightning. Lightning travelling through the air makes the bang of thunder. We see the lightning before we hear the thunder. This is because the speed of light is much quicker than the speed of sound.

BE SAFE IN A THUNDERSTORM!

- Stay indoors, or in a car (but don't touch its sides).
- Don't use the Internet or telephone.
- If you are outdoors, don't shelter under a tree. Lightning strikes tall objects.
- Because lightning strikes tall things, get closer to the ground than the nearest object.

Fog and visibility

Fog and mist are also types of cloud. When the air is full of **water vapour**, some of it will become water droplets. These form around tiny bits of dirt in the air. Fog often occurs in the mornings or evenings, until the warmth of the sun **evaporates** it. The water droplets in fog are the same size as those in cloud. The water droplets in mist are much finer. This is the reason why mist is not as thick as fog. If you cannot see as far as 1 kilometre (0.6 miles) away you are in fog, but if you can see further, you are in mist.

Four kinds of fog-type clouds

Radiation fog is caused when the air above rivers, lakes and valley bottoms cools down to the point where the water in the air **condenses** (called the dew point), and becomes fog. This type of fog often happens on cool, clear nights when the heat has left the ground. If the weather stays cool it can last for days, but in sunny weather it is cleared by the warmth of the Sun's rays.

The cooling of air near the surface of the water produces this radiation fog. If it gets warmer, it will soon disappear.

Advection fog (sometimes called sea fog) is created when warm moist air travels over a cold land surface. It also occurs when the same type of air passes over a cold current at sea. This fog does not rise above about 500 metres (1,640 feet) from the ground, as the temperature starts to get warmer above this. This is why the top of the Golden Gate Bridge often peeps out over the top of the fog in San Francisco, California, USA.

Steam fog, or "arctic sea smoke", is the result of cold air hanging over warm water. For this fog to form, there needs to be a temperature difference of at least 10 °C (50 °F) between the air and the water. This fog is seen a lot in the Arctic, as very cold air blows over warmer water until the water seems to steam. It can also be seen on roads that are warmed by the Sun after a sudden shower of rain.

When there is a lot of pollution in the air, a nasty type of fog called smog is produced. The only way to stop smog is to control chemical **emissions** from vehicles and factories.

Four types of fog				
	When	**Where**	**Air/surface conditions**	**Wind**
Radiation fog	Night-time	Rivers, valleys, low places, not over sea	Cooling ground, moist air	Light breeze
Advection fog (sea fog)	Daytime	At sea	Warm moist air over cold surface	Gentle wind
Steam fog	When there is at least 10°C (50°F) difference between water and air	The Arctic, on sun-warmed roads	Cold air over warm water	Still air
Smog	When smoke and pollutants are present in the air	Industrial areas	Layer of warm air over layer of cold air	Still air

Glossary

air mass body of air in which all the air is of approximately the same temperature and humidity

air pressure pressure at the surface of the Earth caused by the weight of the air in the atmosphere

atmosphere the gases that surround our planet. They are kept in place by Earth's gravity.

big bang theory which states that the universe began in a huge explosion

cirrus highest form of clouds, made up of ice crystals in thin feather-like shapes

climate the pattern of weather over a long period of time

condensation water that has changed from a gas into a liquid, or the process of changing from gas into liquid

condenses when a gas turns into a liquid

convectional vertical movement, especially upwards, of warm air

convergence meeting at one point

cumulonimbus A giant cumulus cloud which rises high in the sky and is often at the centre of a rain and lightening storm

cumulus kind of cloud consisting of rounded heaps with a flat bottom

data facts that can be investigated to get information

emissions things that come out of something

equator imaginary line around the centre of the Earth, at equal distance from the north and south poles

evaporate when water changes from a liquid into water vapour

fossil fuels natural fuel such as coal, oil, and natural gas

greenhouse effect gases which act as a kind of insulator, stopping the Earth's warmth from escaping. The term is also used to describe the increase in gases that has caused too much heat to be kept in the atmosphere, warming the Earth.

halo circle of light around a light source

hoar frost ice which forms on surfaces near the ground when the temperature falls below zero

ice crystal small piece of frozen water which has a regular shape

incus Latin word for anvil – an iron block on which metals are hammered out. It is used to describe the flattened, anvil-like shape at the top of some cumulonimbus clouds.

meteorologists people who study the weather by gathering and analysing data

nimbus large grey cloud that brings rain

overcast when the sky is completely covered in cloud

pileus Latin for soft felt cap (a hat). A pileus cloud has the shape of a flat cap and occurs at the top of, or above, some cumulonimbus clouds.

polar to do with the north or south pole

poles imaginary points opposite each other. They are found at the most northern and southern points of the Earth. Both have very cold climates.

precipitation moisture that falls from clouds in a variety of forms, for example rain, snow, and hail.

radiation type of energy

sphere round, ball-like shape

stratus type of cloud made up of layers, with a flat base

thermal current of rising heat

tropical to do with the region around the equator

turbulence when air moves around, causing winds and draughts

updraught rising current of air

water vapour water in the form of gas

weather front where air masses of different temperatures and humidity meet. This is often the place where the most significant weather happens.

Find out more

You will have read about the greenhouse effect (page 9). Do you know about global dimming? This is a new theory which has yet to be proved. Find out about this interesting theory and see what your conclusion is when you have read the evidence.

Become a cloud spotter! Make a cloud collection. Photograph as many different types of cloud as you can. You can make them into your own reference book and put them into a digital presentation to share with others. (Remember not to look directly at the Sun.)

Websites

http://www.cloudappreciationsociety.org/
The Cloud Appreciation Society has been developed by people keen on clouds. They share photographs, ideas, and weblinks.

http://www.metoffice.gov.uk/publications/clouds/
The UK Meteorological Office has lots of information to help cloud spotters.

http://www.wildwildweather.com/clouds.htm
On Wildwildweather.com you can find photographs which will help you classify the clouds you see. Try to make your collection this good.

More books to read

A Key to the Clouds, Lee Swain and Malcolm Walker
   (The Royal Meteorological Society, 2001)
Weather, Derek Elsom (Marshall Editions, 1998)
Discovering Geography: Weather, Rebecca Hunter (Raintree, 2003)

Index

Cut, Paste, and Create

Cut and Paste

Farm Animals

Rosie Hankin

GARETH**STEVENS**
GS
PUBLISHING
A Member of the WRC Media Family of Companies

Thank you Ottilie, Freddie, Idina, and Sylvia for your help and inspiration.

Please visit our web site at: **www.garethstevens.com**
For a free color catalog describing Gareth Stevens Publishing's
list of high-quality books and multimedia programs, call
1-800-542-2595 (USA) or 1-800-387-3178 (Canada).
Gareth Stevens Publishing's fax: (414) 332-3567

Library of Congress Cataloging-in-Publication Data available upon
request from publisher. Fax (414) 336-0157 for the attention of
the Publishing Records Department.

ISBN-13: 978-0-8368-7719-9 (lib. bdg.)

This North American edition first published in 2007 by
Gareth Stevens Publishing
A Member of the WRC Media Family of Companies
330 West Olive Street, Suite 100
Milwaukee, Wisconsin 53212 USA

This U.S. edition copyright © 2007 by Gareth Stevens, Inc. Original edition
copyright © 2005 by Haldane Mason Ltd. First published in 2005 by Red Kite Books,
an imprint of Haldane Mason Ltd., P.O. Box 34196, London NW10 3YB, United Kingdom.
(info@haldanemason.com)

All original artwork by Rosie Hankin.

Gareth Stevens editor: Barbara Kiely Miller
Gareth Stevens designer: Kami Strunsee

Printed in Canada

1 2 3 4 5 6 7 8 9 10 10 09 08 07 06

 Contents

Craft A-B-Cs

Making things with paper, cardboard, paste or glue, and other craft materials is lots of fun! You will be surprised at what you can make when you start to cut, paste, and create!

Making Cut-and-Paste Crafts!

You can make the fun crafts in this book using simple materials that you cut up and then paste or stick together. To get started, choose a craft, then collect and prepare the materials you need. Next, read through the instructions and look at the picture of the finished project. The picture shows you how to paste all the pieces together to create a work of art. If some steps are too difficult for you, ask a grown-up for help.

You do not need to be an artist to make fun and interesting crafts. You only need to cut and paste different shapes. Each project in this book uses simple shapes such as circles, squares, rectangles, and triangles. The shapes you need for each project are shown in the book. Each shape has a number on it. The number tells you how many pieces of that shape you need to make. The shapes also have names to help you fit them together.

All the shapes are easy to draw or trace. To trace a shape, place a sheet of tracing paper on top of a page in the book. Tracing paper is very thin, white paper you can see through. Use a pencil to draw the outline of a shape on the tracing paper. Cut out the shape you have drawn. Use this shape as a pattern, or template, to draw the shape on colored paper or cardboard. You can make your shape the same size or bigger or smaller than the shape in the book.

To make each craft in this book, first draw and cut out all the pieces, then follow the numbered instructions and look at the pictures to learn how to paste or glue them in place. Your finished craft does not have to look exactly like the picture. You can create each craft your own way. Look in the book for **Bright Ideas!** to make your craft even more special.

Shapes such as circles are hard to draw well, but you can find many round objects to draw around: coins, glasses, cups, plates, and bowls. Look around for objects with other shapes, such as ovals, that might be useful in drawing the shapes needed for these projects.

Once you have tried some of the ideas in this book, you will be able to dream up your own works of art.

Look through old magazines and cut out pictures of things to use in your craft projects. You could even include a photo of yourself or a friend. If your family has a digital camera, ask one of your parents to print out photos you can use. Never cut up a magazine or a photo, however, without asking a grown-up first!

Craft Materials
· · · · · · · · · · · · · · · · · · ·

For all the crafts in this book, you need a pencil, a ruler, scissors with rounded tips, and white paste, glue, or a glue stick. Each craft has a list of the other materials you will need. Most of the crafts use thick, colored construction paper or thin, colored cardboard. You may also need paper plates and bowls, stickers, and clear tape.

Kinds of Paper
· · · · · · · · · · · · · · · ·

The colored paper and cardboard used for these crafts are the kind you probably have at school or at home. Special kinds of paper are also needed for some of the crafts. Adhesive paper is like a sticker. You peel the adhesive paper away from its paper backing and press it down to make it stick. Tissue paper is thin, soft paper that usually comes in large, folded sheets. Corrugated paper has a lot of ridges and grooves. Crepe paper is stretchy paper that comes in many colors. Aluminum foil is shiny paper that looks like a thin sheet of metal. You probably have aluminum foil in your kitchen.

The instructions for each craft tell you to use certain colors of paper or cardboard, but you can use any colors you like. If the only paper or cardboard you have is white, you can color it yourself with crayons or colored pencils or markers. You can even paint it.

Finding Supplies

You do not have to buy all the supplies you need for these projects. You can sometimes find colored paper in old magazines and can use the cardboard from packages such as cereal boxes. Ask your parents if they have scraps of fabric, yarn, and other small items you can use. You can create works of art with things you find lying around your own home, such as cardboard tubes from empty rolls of paper towels or toilet paper. Always ask a grown-up if it is okay to cut up or use any materials before you begin.

Staying Safe

To stay safe while you cut and paste, always use scissors with rounded tips when you need to cut things. If you have trouble cutting cardboard with your safe scissors, ask a grown-up to cut it for you with sharper scissors or a knife. Use only paints, felt-tip pens, and glues that are nontoxic, which means they are safe for kids. You may get glue or paint on your fingers, so keep your hands away from your face until after you wash them.

Making a Mess and Cleaning Up

Creating crafts almost always means making a mess. Before you begin, cover your work surface with old newspapers or a tablecloth that can be wiped clean. Wear an apron or an old shirt to protect your clothes, and roll up your sleeves. If you are painting, use water bowls with wide bases so they do not tip over. Fill up a sink with warm, soapy water so it is ready for washing your hands, paintbrushes, paint jars, and other tools. When you have finished working, pick up and put away all the materials you were using. Now everything will be ready for the next time you want to cut, paste, and create.

Big Red Tractor

You will need:

- red, white, black, and dark green paper or cardboard
- background cardboard (any color)
- 1 round black sticker
- 1 round yellow sticker

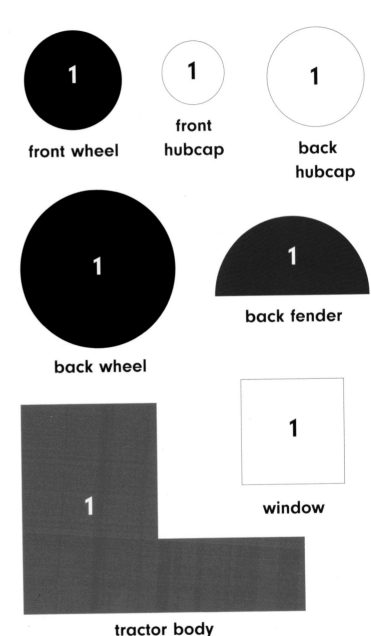

1
front wheel

1
front hubcap

1
back hubcap

1
back wheel

1
back fender

1
window

1
tractor body

1 Cut an L shape for the tractor body out of red paper or cardboard.

2 Cut a square window out of white paper or cardboard.

3 Cut a large circle and a medium-sized circle for the back and front wheels out of black paper or cardboard. Then, cut a medium-sized circle and a small circle for the back and front hubcaps out of white paper or cardboard.

8

This picture of the tractor shows you how to paste all the pieces together. Get ready to start plowing!

Bright Ideas!
- Paste the tractor onto a cardboard tube from an empty roll of toilet paper to make it stand up.
- In the window, draw a picture of a farmer driving the tractor or paste a photo or a magazine picture there.

4 Cut a large semicircle for the back fender out of dark green paper or cardboard.

5 Paste the body of the tractor onto the background cardboard. Paste the window onto the top part, or cab, of the tractor body.

6 Paste the black wheels onto the tractor. Put the bigger wheel at the back. Paste a hubcap onto each wheel. Paste the green fender over the top of the back wheel.

7 Stick half of a round black sticker on top of the front part of the tractor body. Stick half of a yellow sticker at the front of the tractor for a light.

9

Duck Pond

You will need:

- blue, yellow, and orange paper or cardboard
- background cardboard (any color)
- orange felt-tip pen
- 2 small, round black stickers or a thick, black felt-tip pen

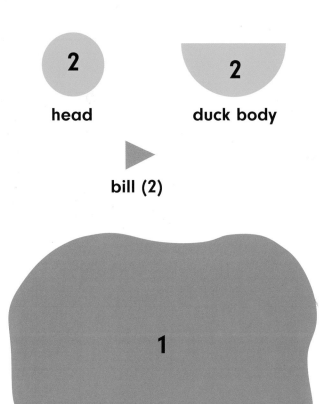

2 head

2 duck body

bill (2)

1

pond

1 Cut a pond shape out of blue paper or cardboard.

2 Cut a large circle out of yellow paper or cardboard. Cut the circle in half to make two large semicircles. Use one semicircle for each duck body.

3 Cut two small circles out of yellow paper or cardboard. Use one circle for each duck's head.

4 Cut two small triangles out of orange paper or cardboard. Use one triangle for each duck's bill.

This picture of the duck pond shows you how to paste all the pieces together. Quack! Quack! Your ducks are ready to swim.

5 Paste the pond shape onto the background cardboard.

6 Paste the two semicircles, or duck bodies, onto the pond shape with the curved sides down. Paste one small, yellow circle at one end of each semicircle.

7 Paste an orange beak onto each duck's head. You could also draw a beak on each duck's head with an orange felt-tip pen.

8 To make eyes, stick a small black sticker on each duck's head or draw the eyes with a black felt-tip pen.

Bright Ideas!
- Make a family of ducks. Make big white ducks and yellow chicks.
- Cut reeds out of green paper or cardboard. Paste them around the edge of the pond.

11

Pink Pig

- pink cardboard (or white cardboard painted pink)
- white paper plate, about 9 inches (22 centimeters) across
- pink paint
- paintbrush
- 4 small, round black stickers
- thick, black felt-tip pen
- 2 large, round white stickers
- hole punch
- pink yarn

1 Cut an oval nose, two ears, and two legs out of pink cardboard.

2 Paint the bottom of a paper plate pink. Let the paint dry.

3 Stick two small, round black stickers onto the nose to make the pig's nostrils. Paste the nose in the middle of the paper plate, on the painted side.

4 Draw a mouth below the nose with a black felt-tip pen.

1

nose

2

leg

2

ear

12

This picture of the pig shows you how all the pieces should be put together. Is your pig smiling? It might be ready to eat or to roll around in the mud!

Bright Ideas!

- Cut out a spiral of pink paper to make a tail.
- Paint the bottoms of two paper plates. Paste or staple the edges together with the painted sides facing outward.
- Use foam stickers to attach the nose so it sticks out from the face.

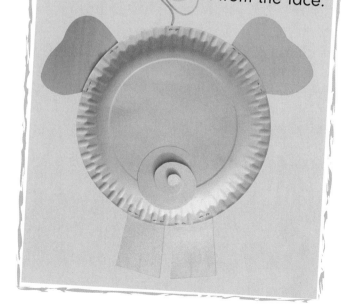

5 To make eyes, stick two large white stickers onto the plate, above the nose. Stick small black stickers on top of the white stickers.

6 Paste the ears onto the top edge of the plate, on the unpainted side.

7 Draw a black line at the bottom of each leg to make toes. Paste the legs onto the bottom edge of the plate, ⬛⬛⬛⬛ painted side.

8 Punch a hole in t⬛⬛⬛⬛⬛plate, between the pig'⬛⬛⬛⬛⬛iece of pink yarn throug⬛⬛⬛⬛ie it to make a loop. Now y⬛⬛⬛⬛your pig.

Cow Mask

You will need:

- white paper plate, about 9 inches (22 cm) across
- hole punch
- black paper or cardboard
- pink paint (or a pink crayon or marker)
- paintbrush
- black tissue paper
- 2 large, round black stickers
- black felt-tip pen
- thin, white elastic

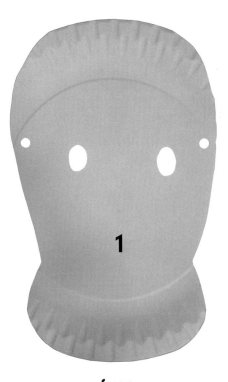

face

1 Cut a face shape out of a white paper plate. Use the leftover pieces of the plate to cut two ear shapes.

2 Hold the face shape up to your face. Ask a grown-up to mark the places on the shape to make two eyeholes. Cut out the eyeholes.

3 Punch a hole on each side of the face shape, just above each eyehole.

4 Cut two or three spot shapes out of black paper or cardboard.

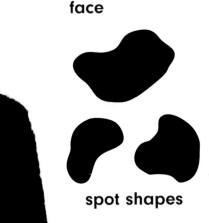

spot shapes

5 Paint the bottom of the face shape pink for the cow's nose. Let the paint dry.

14

This picture of the cow mask shows you how all the pieces fit together. Will your friends know who you are when you wear the mask?

Bright Idea!
Make the cow's hair by cutting long pieces of black yarn. Tie the pieces together in the middle, then paste them onto the top of the cow's head.

6 Paste the ears onto the back of the face shape, at the top, and paste the black spots onto the front of the face.

7 Scrunch up black tissue paper to make hair. Paste it onto the top of the cow's head.

8 Use black stickers to make nostrils on the nose. Draw a smile with a black felt-tip pen.

9 Ask a grown-up to pull elastic through the punched holes and tie it so it fits around your head.

Fluffy Rabbit

You will need:

- pink paper or cardboard
- green background cardboard
- 1 cotton ball
- 2 large, round white stickers
- 2 small, round black stickers
- 1 large, round black sticker

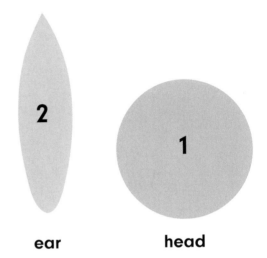

ear   head

1 Cut two ear shapes out of pink paper or cardboard.

2 Cut two round circles out of pink paper or cardboard. The circle for the rabbit body should be larger than the circle for the head. To make the circles, find two round objects, such as a cup and a saucer. Draw around them to make the shapes.

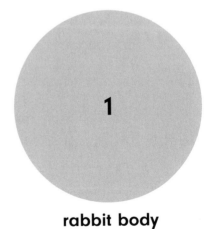

rabbit body

3 Paste the rabbit body near the bottom of the background paper or cardboard.

4 Paste the head onto the top of the body.

This picture of the rabbit shows you how all the pieces fit together. Will your rabbit hop into a farmer's vegetable patch to snack on some carrots?

Bright Ideas!
- Bend one of the ears so it flops forward.
- Make whiskers out of yarn and draw on a mouth.
- Shred green tissue paper to make grass. Paste it at the bottom of the picture.

5 Paste the ears onto the head. Tuck them behind the head if you can.

6 Add a tail by pasting a white cotton ball onto the body.

7 To make the rabbit's eyes, stick two round white stickers onto the middle of the head. Stick small black stickers onto the white stickers. Use a large black sticker for the rabbit's nose.

Meadow Flower

- orange, dark green, and yellow paper or cardboard
- light green background cardboard

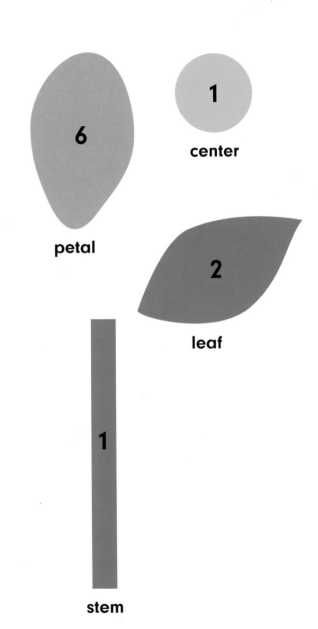

petal

center

leaf

stem

1 Cut six petal shapes out of orange paper or cardboard.

2 Cut a long stem and two leaf shapes out of dark green paper or cardboard.

3 Cut a circle for the center of the flower out of yellow paper or cardboard.

4 Paste the stem onto light green background cardboard.

5 Paste the petals in a circle at the top of the stem.

18

This picture of the flower shows you how all the pieces should be pasted together. Will your flower bring butterflies and honeybees to the meadow?

Bright Idea!
Make a meadow of flowers by cutting simple flower shapes out of paper of many different colors. Paste two leaves onto the back of each flower shape, then paste the flowers onto background cardboard. Use round yellow stickers for the centers of the flowers.

6 Paste the yellow center in the middle of the petals.

7 Paste one leaf on each side of the stem, at the bottom.

Woolly Sheep

- black and pink paper or cardboard
- green background cardboard
- 2 large, round white stickers
- 2 small, round black stickers or a black felt-tip pen
- white cotton balls

head

leg

nose (1)

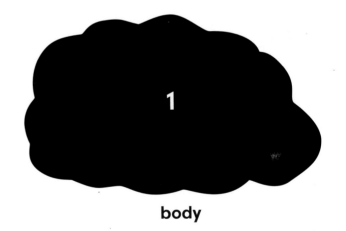

body

1 Cut one head, one body, and four leg shapes out of black paper or cardboard.

2 Cut a small nose shape out of pink paper or cardboard.

3 Paste the body shape onto the middle of the background cardboard.

4 Paste the head and leg shapes onto the background cardboard.

20

This picture of the sheep shows you where to paste all the pieces. Do you know the words to the nursery rhyme "Baa, Baa, Black Sheep"?

Bright Ideas!
- Give your sheep a fluffy cotton-ball head and tail.
- Use shredded green tissue paper to add some grass.

5 Paste the pink nose onto the head, near the bottom.

6 To make the sheep's eyes, use white stickers. Then, stick small black stickers in the middle of the white stickers. You can use a black felt-tip pen instead of small black stickers for the eyes, too.

7 Paste cotton balls all over the sheep's body to make its wool.

21

Clucking Hen

- white, yellow, orange, and red paper or cardboard
- background cardboard (any color)
- 1 small, round black sticker

1 Cut an egg shape out of white paper or cardboard.

2 Cut a body shape and a round head out of yellow paper or cardboard. Use round objects to help you draw the shapes.

3 Cut a wing shape and a triangle beak shape out of orange paper or cardboard.

4 Cut a comb shape out of red paper or cardboard. (Use the same round object to draw the base of the comb that you used to draw the head.)

22

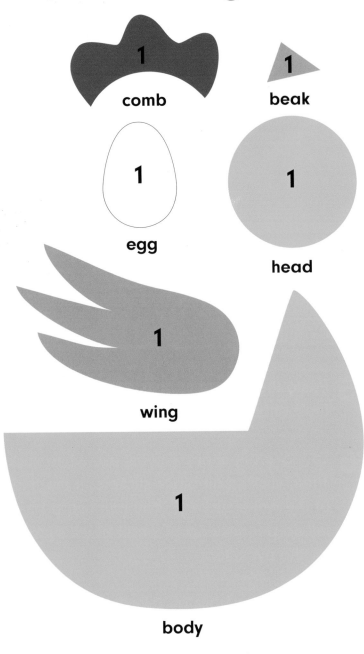

comb

beak

egg

head

wing

body

This picture of the hen sitting on her egg shows you how to put all the pieces together. Will a chick hatch out of your hen's egg?

5 Paste the body shape onto background cardboard. Then, paste on the head.

6 Paste the red comb above the head and paste the orange beak in front of the head.

7 Paste the egg shape at the back of the body with part of the egg on the background cardboard. Paste the wing shape onto the body, covering the top edge of the egg.

8 Stick a black sticker onto the head to make the hen's eye.

Bright Ideas!
• Paste feathers that you find or buy onto the hen's body to make the wing.
• Shred some tissue paper to make straw for the hen to sit on.

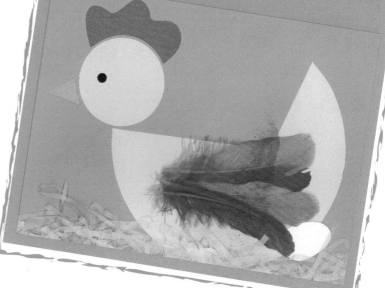

Fish Pond

You will need:

- large sheet of blue paper or cardboard
- red, pink, orange, yellow, and green paper or cardboard
- black felt-tip pen
- 5 paperclips
- small square of thin cloth
- magnet
- string
- straight wooden stick, about 24 inches (60 cm) long

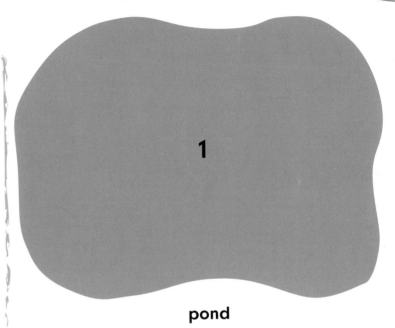

pond

1 Cut a large pond shape out of blue paper or cardboard.

2 Cut the shapes for five fish bodies and five triangular fins out of red, pink, orange, yellow, and green paper or cardboard.

3 Paste one fin onto each fish body. Draw an eye on each fish with a black felt-tip pen.

4 Attach a paperclip mouth to the head of each fish.

fish body

fin (5)

24

This picture of the fish pond shows you where to put the fins and paperclips on the fish shapes. How many fish do you think you will catch with your fishing pole?

5 To make a fishing pole, wrap a small square of cloth around a magnet and tie the cloth closed tightly with one end of a long piece of string. Tie the other end of the string to a long stick.

6 Lay the fish on the blue pond shape. Use the fishing pole to catch the fish. The metal paperclips will stick to the magnet hanging from the fishing pole.

Bright Idea!
Decorate the pond with flowers. (See page 19.)

 # Apple Tree

You will need:

- green cardboard
- cardboard tube from an empty roll of toilet paper
- brown paint
- paintbrush
- 16 or more round red stickers

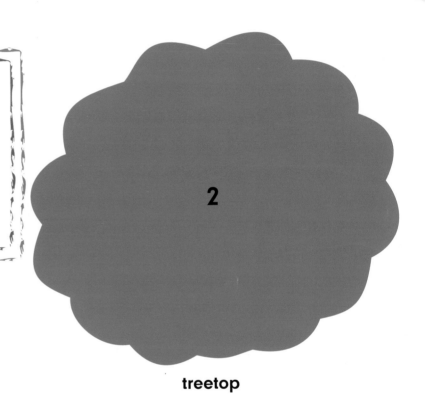

treetop

1 Cut two treetop shapes out of green cardboard.

2 To make a tree trunk, paint the outside of a cardboard tube brown. Let the paint dry.

3 Stick eight or more red stickers all over one side of each green treetop shape. The red stickers are the tree's apples.

This picture of the apple tree shows you how all the pieces should fit together. Will you eat your apples right off the tree or bake a pie with them?

Bright Idea!

Make an orchard of fruit trees. Make the treetops different shapes and different shades of green. Make different kinds of fruits by cutting small pieces of colored cardboard or pasting on tissue paper balls.

4 Paste one treetop shape onto one side of the tree trunk. The apples on the treetop should face away from the trunk. Stick the second treetop shape onto the other side of the tree trunk. The apples on the second treetop should also face away from the trunk.

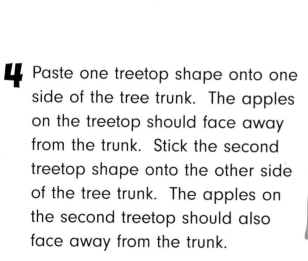

27

Windmill

You will need:

- light gray, blue, red, and yellow paper or cardboard
- background cardboard (any color)

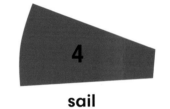

center   **roof**

sail

1 Cut the large, four-sided shape for the base of the windmill out of light gray paper or cardboard. Make the top of the shape narrower than the bottom.

2 Cut a triangle roof and a rectangle door out of blue paper or cardboard.

3 Cut four sails, or blades, out of red paper or cardboard.

4 Cut a small circle for the center of the sails out of yellow paper or cardboard.

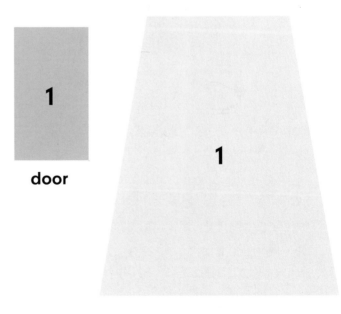

door

windmill base

This picture of the windmill shows you how all the pieces should be pasted together. Imagine the *sails* on your windmill twirling around on a windy day!

Bright Ideas!

- Make your windmill stand up! Paste all the pieces together, then use paste and clear tape to attach the windmill to the cardboard tube from an empty roll of toilet paper.
- Make the sails separately, gluing a center circle on the front and on the back. Attach the sails to the base shape with a brass paper fastener so the sails can spin around.

5 Paste the base of the windmill onto the background cardboard. Paste the roof and the door onto the base shape.

6 Paste the four red sails onto the front of the windmill, close to the roof.

7 Paste the yellow circle in the center of the sails.

Scarecrow

- red, yellow, orange, and brown paper or cardboard
- black corrugated paper
- background cardboard (any color)
- thick, black felt-tip pen
- 3 large, round purple stickers

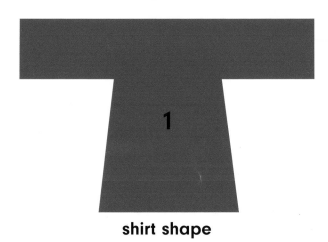

hat

nose (1)

post

head

shirt shape

1 Cut a T-shaped shirt out of red paper or cardboard.

2 Cut a round head out of yellow paper or cardboard.

3 Cut a small, carrot-shaped nose out of orange paper or cardboard.

4 Cut a hat shape out of brown paper or cardboard.

5 Cut a post out of black corrugated paper.

This picture of the scarecrow shows how all the pieces fit together. Is your scarecrow scary enough to put out in a farm field?

Bright Ideas!
- Make your scarecrow's shirt out of a piece of fabric and add a feather to the hat.
- Cut the shapes of flying crows out of black paper or cardboard. Paste the crows above the scarecrow.
- Shred green tissue paper to paste at the bottom of the post for plants.

6 Paste the shirt shape onto the middle of the background cardboard. Paste the head above the shirt and paste the post below the shirt.

7 Paste the orange nose onto the head. Draw crosses on the head with a black felt-tip pen to make eyes.

8 Paste the hat at the top of the head. Stick three purple stickers on the shirt for buttons.

31

More Craft Books

Crafts for Little Kids (101 really, really, really fun ideas!). (Better Homes & Gardens)

Things to Make and Do. Usborne Farmyard Tales (series). Anna Milbourne (Usborne Books)

I Can Make That! Fantastic Crafts for Kids. Mary Wallace (Maple Tree Press)

Sing! Play! Create! Hands-on Learning for 3- to 7-year-olds. Lisa Boston (Williamson Publishing)

Craft Web Sites

Farm Crafts
www.enchantedlearning.com/crafts/farm/

ZOOMdo: Get artsy! Get crafty!
pbskids.org/zoom/activities/do/

Publisher's note to educators and parents: Our editors have carefully reviewed these Web sites to ensure that they are suitable for children. Many Web sites change frequently, however, and we cannot guarantee that a site's future contents will continue to meet our high standards of quality and educational value. Be advised that children should be closely supervised whenever they access the Internet.